Waco Cultural Arts Fest

WordFest Anthology 2017

Edited by
Sandi Horton

Cover Art: Mark Kieran

Front: "Mind's Eye"
(36' x 48' acrylic and oil on canvas)

Back: "Springtime in the Himalayas and the Mystic Crow" (36' x 48' oil on masonite)

Mind's Eye is my representation of a mindscape, if you will, the narrative that we have compiled over time. We all have a story and we peer out into the universe interpreting our surroundings, events, people, and even ourselves. This painting was inspired by a particular person who remains special to me.

Springtime in the Himalayas and the Mystic Crow
As we travel through this journey we call 'our life' we sometimes experience long winters -- maybe hardship, loss, or loneliness. But the blossoming flowers of spring always come. I think the Mystic Crow knows this. When I get a chance to observe a crow close up, I'm struck with how intelligent they truly are and sometimes imagine that they "know."

Mark Kieran

Mark Kieran is an award winning surrealist, abstract, and visionary artist currently residing in Central Texas. He finds inspiration for his work in nature, music, and meditation. Mark fuses ideas, philosophy, and spiritualism with his art.

WordFest Anthology 2017

Every poem in this anthology represents the unique talent of the poet who composed it. A multitude of subjects are present, in a variety of styles, written by poets of all ages from teen-agers to octogenarians.

This anthology features some of the best poets in Texas including two former Texas Poets Laureate Karla K. Morton (2010) and Alan Birkelbach (2005), plus former Oklahoma Poet Laureate Nathan Brown (2013-14). Karla is the Feature Poet for WordFest in 2017. Nathan will be the WordFest Feature Poet in 2018.

Poets from Washington State to Washington D.C. have been selected for this anthology. In addition to American poets from coast to coast, international poets from Australia and Ireland are included.

This diverse collection of 21st century poems will give readers a new way to see the world and its inhabitants.

"Traveling Twosome" (Photo by Ysabel de la Rosa)

From the editor of *WordFest Anthology 2017*

Compiling, formatting, typing, and/or editing over 10,000 words is a time-consuming process. It is a labor of love to honor fellow writers by publishing their poems in this anthology.

A special thank you to Doreen Ravenscroft, Chris Boldt, and Jeff Horton for helping with this anthology and with WordFest.

May we always remember the value of our poems whether written or spoken.

Bleeding Pen

There is power in words
Power to hurt
Power to heal

May my pen bleed words
Full of compassion
To cleanse wounds

Apply fresh bandages
So healing can begin
With life giving ink

Sandi Horton, editor

WORDFEST SCHEDULE 2017

(Most events are in Waco Convention Center, Level 1))

Friday, Oct. 6

7-9 p.m.　　**Open mic** *(for all ages)*
　　　　　　Host:　Mary Evans

Saturday, Oct. 7

9:30-11 a.m.　**Location:　Armstrong Browning Library (ABL) on the Baylor University Campus**

Open mic/Gathering of poets in the Garden of Meditation (Poet's Park) located on the ABL grounds

Guided tour of the ABL

1-2 p.m.　　**Workshop:　Talking Back to Poetry**
　　　　　　Presenters:　Joyce and Mike Gullickson

2-3 p.m.　　**FEATURE POET Reading**
　　　　　　Karla K. Morton
　　　　　　2010 Texas Poet Laureate

3-4 p.m.　　**Workshop:　Turning Your Fortune Into Poetry**
　　　　　　Presenter:　Karla K. Morton

6-7 p.m.　　**Distinguished Writers' Reception** *(by invitation)*Entertainment by Katie Stewart

7-9 p.m.　　**Anthology Reading** *(open to the public)*
　　　　　　Host:　Karla K. Morton

Sunday, Oct. 8

12-1 p.m. **Workshop – Making Every Submission Count: Improve Your Acceptance Rate**
Presenter: Ann Howells

2-3 p.m. **Writers Panel: Karla K. Morton, Ann Howells, Joyce and Mike Gullickson**
Host: Sandi Horton

3-5 p.m. **Open Mic** (for all ages)

"A Feather on the Breath of God,"
phrase by Abbess Hildegard of Bingen
(Photo by Ysabel de la Rosa)

WordFest Anthology Poems

WordFest Anthology 2017

Moments

Precious are
stolen moments
of forbidden love

snatched
from sullen heft
of life's dull days

tucked
between pages
of reflection

bundled nimbus
lipped
as exquisite wine

Kaye Voigt Abikhaled
West Lake Hills, Texas

Defining a Poet

She asked me to define a poet
but I didn't have an answer
at the time. So here's my
more considered definition:
A poet fishes in the sea
of our collective unconscious
for deep-swimming idea fishes,
using pieces of his own
gut for bait.
A poet must lie to tell the truth
that we don't want to acknowledge,
and might never otherwise acquire.
A poet squeezes your heart
like a sponge for emotions
you may fear, but need, to feel.
A poet makes your mind itch
and your neurons snap like
downed power lines writhing
and sparking in a storm.
A poet transforms words to wonder
as Jesus changed water to wine.
A poet shows you the hole
in your soul then
hands you a shovel.

Michael Baldwin
Benbrook, Texas

Spangles, Cancer's Thin Breath (Two Senyru)

spangles
bursting in air
a soldier kneels

cancer's thin breath
we follow the slip
of her lips

Jan Benson
Fort Worth, Texas

Two Poets over Brunch

A red traffic light and a man on the corner, waiting
I answered her question
as we looked out the deli window
onto a rainy morning
I see more, she said,
then proceeded to describe
birds playing gleefully among the wet leaves of a tree
the way children play in the rain, oblivious
to the wet and their mother's voices
calling for them that it's time to come in
And how cars passing by
were distorted by the wet glass
and how the face of the tower clock across the way
came straight out of a Dali painting, and
if I looked hard enough
I could see more, too
So, I looked again out into the rainy morning
No, I said,
today there's just a red traffic light and
a man on the corner, waiting

Chris Billings
Schertz, Texas

In My Sleep

While lying here
Asleep words are traveling through my mind
I reach for the light switch
Grab paper and pen
       POOOOOOOF
The words are no longer there
They just stopped moving
My thoughts are empty
It's like the words were only in my dreams
Now I try to recapture my words
By going back to sleep
Instead I toss and turn
The words are no longer there
I'm wide awake
Lost in thought
Lost in memory

Lost in words

For the words that were traveling in my sleep have
disappeared

Just as my dreams have disappeared

They no longer exist.

Birdman 313
Houston, Texas

Nature Deficit

The Composer Lady said she'd never heard
of The Music of the Spheres.

Even at fifty years old
that was at least six hundred full moons,
all of them evidently either atonal.
Or unseen.

During the day did she not hear the soft adagio
of the sun passing, the tympani of the moon pulling,
pulling?

On any nights sitting on her perfectly painted and
webbed
chaise-lounge, the reflected light of Mars bathing her
face,
did some deep part of her
not feel the yearning of a vast and fixed calculation?

I suppose on the meteor shower nights,
multiple times a year, any year, all years,
she was at her bound and metered keyboard
counting eights and fifths and demisemiquavers.

As a remedy someone who loves her should lead her
to a pump-well out by a cabin in a quiet wood.
And that person should work the handle
until the liquid is compelled up.
And that person should take that composer's hands
and put them in the flow and say,
"Now. At least.
Feel, feel this heartbeat."

Alan Birkelbach
Lewisville. Texas

For Hope and Mrs. Oliphant

What happiness is not purchased with more or less of
pain?

Margaret Oliphant, Scottish novelist, 1828-1899

When the cataclysms happen
perturbing humankind or krill,
upending the flat land,
crumbling the thrill,
contorting the seas,
and filling them with swill,
we write to round the world again,
to smooth its folds. And still,

the corpse of a love or a child,
brightly-burnished by our words,
laid in galley sheets,
proofed, hardbound, and blurbed,
is never interred.
Our pain is only slurred.
Earthquakes can never be exiled.
We can't write sorrow cured.

The wonder is, I thought that you should know,
my pain is eased by having told you so.

Christine H. Boldt
Temple, Texas

Remains

Bless all the ghost towns
in the American Southwest

for having done all they could
to hold onto the worn-out
reins of their dying horse.

The past dreams of escape
and conquer by the rugged,
who drove stakes down into
the middle of these nowheres
and brought saloons to slake
the hard thirst of desolation.

In the end, we had to have
our Walmarts and Thai food.

But, long after the great cities
have been bombed into oblivion,
these small ruins of towns will…
like scorpions and cockroaches…
continue to haunt this world.

Nathan Brown
Wimberley, Texas

Pale Grasshopper

Moving her forearms together in prayer
she kneels, closes her eyes, listens
to sounds of the outside world recede.

Her life tells of enormous fields
of attention, her face of time not idle.
Its expression floats blessedness.

Rising like a swan, wings graceful
as if worries are being flung away
she gazes toward something precious.

Claire Vogel Camargo
Austin, Texas

The Innocent Howler

In the night, when I am left alone to my own thoughts,
I listen for the distant howl of a friend long vanished,
With the hopes that they are calling my name in the vast
darkness.
"Forgive me for the crimes I have not done."

But still, I know, that wherever they are,
That wolf who thinks they are an Alpha due to their
abilities,
They are suffering.
So am I. I feel no shame in feeling happy for their
downfall.
"Forgive me for the crimes I have not done."

But I am a faithful follower of an Alpha long gone,
One who left their heart open to let me follow their paw
prints on the moist ground.
I love that Alpha with all my heart and back
Because they are family.
I followed the imposter thinking that they too are family,
I was wrong.
"Forgive me for the crimes I have not done."

They kicked me out
And I fell from the heaven and hit the earth with a yelp
Still walking with a limp and sore heart.
That's why I listen into the night.

To the Alphas and the ones who think they are such,
"Forgive me for the crimes I have not done,
I will always forgive you before the moon will set every
dawn."

Derby Carlson, age 16, Waco High School
Waco, Texas

Autopsy

My body found
on the black

sand of a crooked beach
sunbaked into blisters.

The coroner's finding:
a fall from a preposterous height

the pockmarks the pecks
of approximately ten thousand birds

but cannot explain
the wings

sprouting from my armpits.

Ken Chau
Melbourne, Australia

After Reading Your Letter

I lie on the hotel bedspread, tracing the rose pattern
through the polyester (vines, thorns, faded bubble gum
petals)
while tracing the splatter of my thoughts, searching
for patterns in the synapses where hide in my brain,
broke plastic alarm flashing fragments--the digital
detritus
of numbers, not time--no time, no phone, no trace
of me but the ones and zeroes scattered by my credit
card.

I lose myself, or you, or both of us, tires tracing grooves
on the gravel dust of the river road, cows staring in dumb
wonder,
impatient tails swatting flies and seconds, each flick
ticking,
stretching the distance between last night and today.
I see them shrink in the rearview mirror and know:
this is a road I travel once, and I leave some part of you
on the far side of the cattle guard, receding.

One lone maple flames red, always the brightest burning
foreshadows the ashes, and I balance on the cliff, kicking
pebbles
and memories, staring across the valley, the period of
your final
sentence, where we stand, opposed, that single dot
containing us,
beginning to end--complete. So when the last pebble
falls,
the earth scoured clean, I release the brake and drive
away.

Diana L. Conces
Round Rock, Texas

Clarity

I raise my weapon
level with my unyielding eyes.
My feet are rooted
to the roughage beneath me.

The trunk of my body is
strong and erect.
My left arm is fully extended
as my right secures the arrow.

My right hand hooks the string
and I pull back.
Breathe in.
Breathe out.

Breathe in.
Clarity.
Breathe out.
Focus.
Breathe in.

RELEASE.

Angelle Conant
Houston, Texas

After a Winter Storm
Arno River

Yellow lightning
inside sullen smudge
of black cloud.

A rage of muddy water
embellished
by sodden bric-a-brac.

Splintered filigree of trees.

Everywhere dark
umbrellas. Wet
shoes. High

behind black,
light blue.
A paler sun.

Sarah Cortez
Houston, Texas

Mama Cures the Skillet

Yellow sizzles on caste-iron black;
The smell of nothing rises
Striking my senses;
Mama stirs the dark plane
Spreading the melting onto the sides,
Humming as the sound falls
Into a quiet smoking of spent Oleo.

She wipes the face of the pan
Blackening a white napkin
Then sets it aside to rest.

I stare in wonder at the aching metal;
Looking to see what it was she had healed.

David E. Cowen
Houston, Texas

Empty Nest

Time for the best?
Let's go for life's zest!

The best of times
To make silly rhymes
We can read anything at anytime
Even stories of dark crime.

A time to recapture peace and quiet.
A time to quit cigarettes and go on a diet.
Let's say hurray and amen
To now and the end;

Then we can shout for joy
For God's baby boy!
He's willing to take all the sin and the pain
To help each of us our souls to gain.

As we burrow within
To acknowledge and repent sin,
We find the 'empty nest' is indeed the best;
We're lovers and seekers on a new quest

Carol Crosthwait
Dallas, Texas

Cosmic Me: A Truth

There's a sway to the beat of the summer cicadas.
Everything is hush and I am in the middle of the
universe.
I am the man hopping a freight train along the US
border.
I am the woman crying in the night over the shattered
window.
It was all an accident committed on purpose anyway.
I am the stars and the slivered, silver moon.
I am the thick velvet summer air stirring all around.
I am a stinging heart pain and I am the thunderous roll of
joy.
I am a thousand rays of light, gamma and infrared.
I am a cosmic explosion of happening, And yet
I am nothing here.
I am everyone and they are me.
I am the breaking of a ten year old whose mom cries and
drinks bitter potion from a red glass all the time.
I am the mercenary, who slays evil and gives solemn
hallelujahs at night.
I am the victor who was wrongfully imprisoned,
And who emerges from concrete to become the smooth
air again.
I am atoms mingling with trees.
I am everything that was and is and will be.
My head does not worry.
My heart does not ache.
It sways with the rhythm of the cicadas, and I am
reminded
I have already died a thousand times
And I am living again.

Susan Duty
Woodway, Texas

I Love How the Sun Tries to Settle Me Down

I do love how the Sun tries to settle me down –
how it teases my eyes to look West,
spilling ink I can think with across the whole sky,
and doing its absolute best

to convince me to follow its radiant path.
By rich reds, yellows, pinks I am blessed.
What unnerves me deserves free expulsion.
As the Sun settles, that's when I rest.

I do love how the Sun seems to settle me down.
In its warm glow, I often do find
that a setting sun seldom looks angry
at any day it left behind.

Nancy Fierstien
Dripping Springs, Texas

.

Believe In Me

Believe in me
And I will walk beside you
Appreciate me
And I will please you
Stir my imagination
And we can fly
Trust in me
And I won't let you down
Suffer with me
And together we will grow
Feel with me
And we will soar
Believe I love you
And warmth and rapture will be ours
Live life with me
NOW...............
Tomorrow may not be ours.

Josephine Forestier
Canberra, Australia

Rough Seas

I manufactured a kinship with the sea:
when the surf slid up the beach,
I read it as affection,
as though it shared with me
a mutual nostalgia. It flirted.

It tweaked my ankles. It matched me:
the arch of shore to the curve
of my lumbar spine, my arms child-wide
before its bowed horizon.
Its beating waves a heart. Salty as my blood.

But when I fell over the rocks,
pulled into the moaning boil
it ignored me, pounded my sinuses, churned:
I found myself an animal whose gifts
of persuasion had no currency.
All I could speak was panic.

My body flailed, it frothed the chemicals,
reached and found nothing to hold—
air like a desperate gift offered and retracted,
offered and retracted—
all of it overlaid by gasp and frenzy—
a slow sense rising: I am all alone.

Between the thrash and spatter,
the suck of the moon, the darkened granite:
I am the thing that breaks.

Erin Fornoff
Dublin, Ireland

DaVerse Lounge

First time eighth-graders are suspicious—
looking for gotcha behind staged lights
but he has written honest lines
and if sixth-graders can own the mic
he'll tamp the quiver in his throat
and read his poem.

Before applause dies away
as he is stepping off the stage
switch switches to belief
knowing we do it all for him—
band   chairs   bussed in audience
to hear his words
and clap just for him.

He's right
except he's wrong—
we really do it
for that eighth-grade day
when we spilled words onto the page
and needed a turn
at mic that wasn't there.

Alan Gann
Dallas, Texas

Nine Hundred Miles

Nine hundred miles ago I knew a man –
we walked the fields; we'd seldom speak.
He'd stare into an approaching dark. I used to stand

the way he stood, tiptoeing to take a peek.
That's how boys would learn from silent men.
We'd walk the fields; we'd seldom speak.

Our chores, the hay, the crops, all kept us busy then
and when I'd tire he'd keep on going.
That's how boys learned from silent men.

Last time we talked I wasn't the same boy growing
up in his house. We pointed out each other's mistakes
and when I tired he'd still be going.

Nine hundred miles to drive and think. My head aches.
I wonder what conspiracy's got him wound up now.
Up in his house, we pointed out each other's mistakes.

Nine hundred miles I hoped the memory'd fade,
somehow
but I'm staring at an approaching dark, trying to make a
stand.
I wonder what conspiracy's got him wound up now --
if he's staring at the approaching dark, where we used to
stand.

Dwight A. Gray
Copperas Cove, Texas

Truth is

In deepest darkness, it's difficult to see,
beauty betrayed, by my own hand.
leaf, storm, feathers
into seed, order, chaos—
into Mother in the garden.
She plants a garden of forgiveness,
Irish potatoes, and tomato seeds

It's difficult to see reasons, and
things that grow in the dark.
Truth is, she remains complicit.
Truth is, we are all deceivers.
Truth is, the beauty of the blank page
waiting for a seed, leaf, feather.
What does it mean to betray?
What does darkness yield?

Joyce Gullickson
Georgetown, Texas

The Last Flash of Sunlight: The Last Roll of Thunder

If my life was done and this poem
was nothing more than a revisiting
of my greatest moments
writing poems/ reading them to you.

I would hum the dirge of lost time
when there was so much left to do
the scars were healed
the greatest failures
now forgotten, now forgiven.

I would listen to the rain
walking on my roof
and write about it
one last time

Michael Gullickson
Georgetown, Texas

Restoration

There's a routine for everything, you know.
The hoarder's apartment will be restored
to pristine condition no matter how many dumpsters
the cleanup crew in their puffy white biohazard suits
have to fill; no matter how many ironing boards and
clothes that almost fit and stacks of newspapers and
used teabags and used toothbrushes and boxes of
Christmas lights and brochures from doctor's offices
have to go; along with the suitcases and cartons of
plastic forks. No matter how many rats and mice and
roaches need to be exterminated and how much mold
needs to be eradicated and smells need to be disinfected
floors that need to be shored up, the crew will eventually
unearth the original configuration of the place; the living
room
couch and kitchen stove and bathroom scale, which will
also
be thrown away. The apartment manager's footsteps will
echo
through the empty rooms, and the walls will glisten. One
day
I'll be emptied of everything that doesn't matter. Then
I'll be able to hear a voice as silent as light; it will call
my name,
and I'll know just what to do.

Kathleen Hart
Longview, Texas

House, Left Unfinished

One day, the workers all packed up and left –
the house's bones exposed, the driveway halfway
paved, garage without a door, a gaping
wound. I pass it on my way to work
each day and wonder why things shrivel up
while others bloom. I wonder if this house
was conceived with great anticipation,
a castle in the sky that fell apart.

I wonder if the wife dreamed of this house
smiling at her with its pearly pickets,
if the husband bought a riding mower,
ready to tend unruly wilderness,
nurture it into a perfect lawn
that he could brag about to everyone.

But there it sits, alone, becoming dust,
returning to the earth like all things do
eventually, this house before its time,
before it had the chance to feel bare feet
against its tiles, to echo laughter, glow
with love at midnight from a bedroom window
as chuck-wills-widows trill their lullabies.

Katherine Hoerth
Beaumont, Texas

Purple

Sometimes my mind
Wanders off the path
And winds up in
A different century

Sometimes I stumble
Into another galaxy
In between time
With colors never imagined

My three year old granddaughter
Tells me that if
You mix Spanish and French
You get purple

Someday she'll be a poet
Travelling between realms
Like her Grammy
And no one can stop us

Sandi Horton
Woodway, Texas

Flyway

Heat waves shimmy our big Chevrolet,
We're going to *the island*, our apartment
sealed tight. Inside carpets curl and brown

as chairs, sofas, beds, form golden crusts.
Dad drives; Mom rides shotgun. Jo-rie and I
share the back, each zealously guarding half.

How much longer? She's on my side!
Then Mom and Dad begin: quiet contralto
harmonizes fluty soprano, melodious

hymns of summer: *Let the Lower Lights
Be Burning, Church in the Wildwood.*
We're entranced by this wonder created

just for us. No longer workaday worms:
our shoulder blades tingle, we emerge
winged creatures whose feet skim the sand.

Ann Howells
Carrollton, Texas

Gestures

Canvas flat and nil,
a brush of dimensional will.
Spiraling lines awaken time.
Saw dust mock-ups arise;
ethereal, material, alive.

A stair case sketch ascends,
erased and drawn again.
Dada déjà vu
enemy-friend figurines.
Plaster bust patterns,
in abstract scenes.

Watercolor dreams
on papier maché.
Foot prints portrayed
in conception or clay;
each masterpiece signed,
the Artist outlines the way.

Lisa Hubley-King
Dripping Springs, Texas

The Fallen Leaf

Here I sit, and I perceive,
the life and death of a fallen leaf.
I was down, my eyes on the ground,
when a leaf fell down without a sound.
A woman walked by on a cell phone,
she stepped on the leaf and had not known.
The leaf still sat on the sidewalk;
it feels no feelings, it cannot talk.
I suppose when I die, I as well;
will no longer have a tale to tell.
Now the wind has blown it away;
it trembles on this autumn day.
As if the leaf is saying goodbye;
I watched the leaf fall down and die.
Another woman walked the path;
stepped on the leaf and started to laugh.
Spring will come and leaves will reappear,
but for this leaf, the end is near.
For this leaf, no one will mourn,
it's only purpose is to be here and warn.
Warning us winter is on its way;
I saw a leaf fall from a tree today.

Mark Hudson
Evanston, Illinois

How I Was Mistaken

Sometimes,
one has to wait for meaning to arrive
like an overdue train, precipitant
in need of a reagent. Or I pour off
what I thought was truth only
to see the silt of misconception
in the bottom of the glass.

The words falter and rearrange themselves
in efforts of knowing.
I am the spear fisher
who misses the fish even though
I have studied refraction.
I shuttle across the hours
in my queer, my variant skin.

Every bend of light that casts
what I see in a color
I'll later rename. Every voice
that calls me out and mistakes me,
every unkind glance mirrored
in my own.

Cindy Huyser
Austin, Texas

Come to Grandmother

Little lost boy.
Rest safely in my arms,
Sleep dear child.

I'll hold you while your parents
Search in vain for the tiny boy
They walked away from in the deep forest.

No bear will harm you as I softly hum a lullaby.

Rosemarie Horvath Iwasa
Garfield Heights, Ohio

War Pies

Bang that pan, whoop and holler.
So what if you're small? Be a bandit, a spy,
a jumping bean. Quick-shinny
that one-pie tree out back and cram
your pail, cherry-full. *Mayday, MAYday!*
Kamikaze crows, at two o'clock,
beaks like triggers—
                    Go, kid,
                    REAP IT, believing
in ovens and frizzled crust, crimson syrup
pulsing through slits. Make a wish
on the point of your slice, but . . .
jangle a tooth on a cherry stone
and Mom collects a kiss, then
rides shotgun, lest anyone dares
backhand your small salute.

Laurie Klein
Deer Park, Washington

Sequestered Sanctuary

While my spouse shopped
for tools, I waited in the car,
saw several sparrows land
atop a small hedge nearby,
disappear into busy green.

As dusk neared and air chilled,
a small flock flew in,
also vanished into the hedge.

More, more, and more came,
until I wondered how many
were cloistered inside,
little brown monks
converging for evening vespers.

Catherine L'Herisson
Garland, Texas

Ironing Silk

this stiff green blouse, crumpled
on the closet floor like an old hankie--
I am going to throw it out, but then I don't.

it is hard to find the iron; I last used it
on a white cotton graduation gown
my daughter wore in kindergarten. She is 50.

the iron still works when I wipe off the cobwebs.
I never could iron, mother tried,
said *do the collar first, then the back,*

then the shoulders. awkwardly I slide
the hot machine over the green silk
and it spreads, widens, smooths.

the blouse is faded in spots but beautiful,
the different greens, the hinted yellows, browns,
and it seems to melt, glow under the iron.

my motions are soothing now, almost skilled,
the harsh bumps relax to gentleness,
oppressed somehow into a glad compliance.

and though when I finish it is still imperfect,
has extra folds, still, it is pliant, soft,
something to wear at summer celebrations.

I hold it up, it billows in the fan,
breathes in the eddies, gestures with sleeves.
light flows over it like liquid love.

Janet McCann
College Station, Texas

Hammock Song

Sunlight sifts through leaves
to write its name on Earth.
A million-mile journey done,
its photons have found a place
to rest—my skin, their Sabbath.

Bone-tired, I feel my aches eased
by the heat that white-washes
my body with speckled light.
Collapsed on the striped canvas
of a hammock, I close my eyes.

With one foot dangling, I nudge
the ground to set my soul in motion:
sway, swing; sway, swing. Riding
the light, I dream of the lovely day
my own journey brought me safely here.

Anne McCrady
Tyler, Texas

That Is Not All

When faded flowers no longer perfume the scent of
summer
and the kaleidoscope of blossoms begin to wither

We know...that is not all

When season's harvest has been gathered
leaving isolated fields of stubble in desolate array

We know...that is not all

When autumn's majesty has become emaciated
until only the skeletal of barren limbs remains

We know...that is not all

Though the earth adorns its desolate shroud
presenting itself as death,
dormant lies the hope through winter's chill
that awaits the breath of spring

Joyce Gorum McGee
Gary, Texas

View from the 14th Floor

Three fertilizer spreaders. Green.
Arranged small to large.
One barbecue grill, red and black.
Sitting on spindly legs.
One pair car ramps. Red.
Displayed to best advantage
For sale on this slow side street.
Tended faithfully each day.
Their sitter in a folding chair.
Are these things the worth of a man?
Is this what remains
After suits have burned his effort?
His life a long ditch, now filled?
A square mile of shingles, now worn?
Are these now his value?
What of despair do I know?
And what does it matter?
What is left at the end of the fall?
A few scraps of cloth, some words.
No spreader
No ramp
No nothing
For sale on this slow side street
To exchange for the worth of a man.

Jay B. McMillen
Waco, Texas

A Breath of New Life

Neighbors said: *Your maple tree looks quite dead!*
Each day they looked at its sheer nakedness,
Anxious like me to see leaves out and spread,
And the twigs sappy, not dry and lifeless.

I thought, *I would miss its foliage beauty*—
Those emerald leaves at the dawn of spring;
And, when in autumn, it dressed festively—
Red, golden leaves spark like bonfire flaming.

But I refused to lose hope on the tree—
It got to wake up from winter slumber!
Like people some trees are slow and dozy,
So I nursed it well with love and prayer.

Then one early morning in late springtime,
I saw tiny leaves sprang out from the tree.
My eyes danced in tears, my heart felt sublime,
God breathed new life into my maple tree.

Sylvia S. Medel
McKinney, Texas

Galactic Rainbows

Existence is…
Contrasting angles,
between transcendence,
and influence.
Choose your own summit,
beyond skyline.
Making footprints in clouds;
spiraling through glowing gases
into Milky Way.
Riding blue-white stars.
Choosing halos around planets,
the galactic rainbows,
to slide into soft lunar dust,
of moons.
To watch supernovas
Light all the galaxy.

Nicole Metts
Copperas Cove, Texas

A Religion of Cicadas

I have witnessed –
seen them rise like souls
from the cracked backs of their bodies,
pale and soft, then meditate
as their skin hardens; darkens.

Thirteen years they've waited
for this moment:
to ascend the branches
where they were conceived,

drawing a deep breath
into cavernous bellies
empty as Monday churches —
built to amplify those accordion ribs...

and sing a song older than Genesis;
a chorus of roar
rivaling every earthly voice.

Days later, spent and sexed,
they fall in revelations
on those brave enough
to bare summer's scald;

bodies delicate as communion wafers;
their clear wings
crystal-thin stained glass
the magic of hallelujah still inside.

Karla K. Morton
Fort Worth, Texas

Landlord

Responsibility without high powers and
Single focus on survival chances
Demanded by my only tenants, the Martins,
Gives this Earth-bound vassal his due labors.
Maintaining a 12-room apartment house,
Fifteen feet above
Becomes a driven task when winds
Blow in gusts
Attacking the dwelling and
Forcing steel to bend.
I worry about my friends
And their home being thrown
Crashing
To the ground!
It would be a wild dash outside
While I attempt to reunite
Egg and nest, sibling to parent,
And at the same time
Reaffirm faith and ask forgiveness.
My reward is their unwavering
Faithfulness spoken in
Vast sweeps of air churned by so
Many dark angel wings as they salute in their attitude of
prayer

Jack Nims
Waco, Texas

My Brain

It is yellow in color....
When that happened, I don't know.
What color was it before?
I don't recall.
But it is yellow now

With blue lines, I think,
Running across its page
And a red line...
A red line running down –
Near but not quite at its left edge.

It contains much that I don't remember:
Pictures, charts and words –
Lots and lots of words.
A date at its top right corner
And calculations on its side.

I lose it a lot these days.
Then wander up and down,
Here and there, out and in,
Till I find it again...
And note down where I lost my brain.

James O. Nyagilo
Dallas, Texas

Last Fall

Tall pine forest limbs tangle the wind
A quiet boring peace repeats each day

Clear valley air between hill sides
speckled with green trees turning orange brown

Suddenly smoke soars smothering the sawmill site
Singing saw blade screeches to a halt

Crackling fire flames flicker
Destruction of property, and lives

Change swept over the town
We could not stop any of it.

Michael Owens
Cypress, Texas

Roses

The rose, romantic
and so beautiful,
admired from afar,
is hard to tend, its thorns
draw blood from careless
ungloved hands. Unlike impatiens,
crepe myrtle in red, white and rosé,
which bloom for months
unserenaded without fail,
roses are gorgeous for a week.
They must be clipped to
force new buds.
Is that why roses are compared
to love? Hard work, scratched skin,
blood streaks, while cutting
out dead blooms and thorny canes?

Christa Pandey
Austin, Texas

A Sizzled Sun

I held my hand to shade my eyes,
as patiently waiting for the sun's
fiery-descent into some far-off water.

I was sure I would hear it sizzle,
or some steam rise off,
from the burning being doused.

If you live on the edge of manifest destiny,
are there any natural boundaries
to hold you back?

It is not just God's hand that can
twist trees or roots, She can also
unclench a wearied-heart.

Life is such a mirage to most of us,
with our noses often pressed to glass,
as the real world rolls by us outside.

Alice Parker
Dallas, Texas

That Observed

It has a short life span, but bright!
It is the lightning bug, surfing
Lazily in summer's twilight.

It lasts what seems forever,
A stone column, perched alone.
It will survive the fires of Rome time and time again.

It comes to you in darkness,
Music emergent, *dolce* —
Without effort from the harp.

It abides in garish light,
Blinding in its goodness,
Never burning, as the sun.

It tumbles over rocks it's smoothed.
Years, from the quiet,
That timid stream, origins up-mountain.

It destroys all
Taking with it the things that stand
In the way of its fatal tide.

It sings,
Only to you.

You shall only hear
When no sound it makes.

B. Rae Perryman
Washington, D.C.

Turn the Page

Neon snowflakes flash on *Lifetime
Fitness*. A musician in high-rise jeans
strums Bob Seger's *Turn the Page* .
Kids run on synthetic turf, kick a scarlet
fluorescent ball. Poplars float
in the fuzzy radiance of lighted garlands.

Her heart beats young, while the black
Garnier dye grows silver roots.
"Here's your ball!" (At home she'll never
stroke the curls of a child like this.)
She hasn't gained life from books
and fruit from faithfulness.

With a cup of minestrone, she stares
at flames of torches – the rusted chalices
hissing in the fountain of Living Water.
"Here I go / Playin' star again."
This pony-tailed guitarist is no Jimmy Page.
He keeps putting his glass on her table.

She leaves, thinking of a job in Maui's
Garden of Eden – a hippy souvenir shop
wrapped in ceaseless rain.

*Elina Petrova
Houston, Texas*

Laura Works at the La Quinta in Rochester Minnesota

Laura does not know it
but while she works at the La Quinta in Rochester
Minnesota,
she lives in the pen of a poet.
A lowly poet who wishes he was a painter,
struggling to reveal her beauty
with brushstrokes, instead of syntax.
She lives in the words of a poet
who yearns to be a sculptor
as to fashion her body in bronze,
hoping to pay tribute to the allure she compels.
She lives in the eye of a poet
who would rather be a photographer,
so as to capture the aura that flits
about the winsomeness that is she.
How could she know, she lives in the mind of this simple
poet?
A poet who aspires to be a philosopher,
grappling to discover at what point
does her inner beauty merge into her outer elegance?
Laura works at the La Quinta in Rochester Minnesota.
Yet that is not ...
all she is.

DaRell Pittman
San Antonio, Texas

Tale of Night

Two dinghies in the night
To our dreams we go,
Slow, tether dragging the slipstream of possibilities.

Our hands have become uncoupled,
Our marriage by day annulled.
Shall I see you yet,
Adrift between exotic places?

I wake to find us
Awash together on calm enough waters,
Both of us starved and weatherworn.

I throw an arm around you.
Dumb with half-sleep I ask you to stay with me.

You answer with your warmth,
Your voice like a log on a fire.

Gerald Plant
Waco, Texas

When Losing Is Winning

I want to be a winner, but lately I've been such a loser.
I've lost unwanted pounds that were making me lazy.
I've lost anger and hostility that made me bitter.
I've lost negativity that pulled me down each day.
I've lost inhibitions that kept me from trying anything
new.

One day, years ago, I lost an engagement.
My world became a dark, gloomy night.
Until the morning came with a move to an exciting city
and I realized the loss was a major gain.

Another day, I lost a job.
My world took on days of uncertainty.
Applications were my life.
Where they fell, I never knew.

Then, just when I thought the word "loser" was coined
for me,
A school hired me and I was back at work.

But, personally, I thought I would live alone forever.
The man I loved seemed out of reach;
arguments ruled our spare moments together.

Then my biggest all-time loss hit me.
The smart, fun man stole my single life.
I lost my loneliness.

Betty Roberts
Denton, Texas

For My Son, on Moving to Phoenix

Let this be a sign to us
that the fire is over
and the ashes are never
too deep to rise from,
no matter how many trees
fell in the burning.

A sign that life, under God,
even after death,
is relivable, and we,
being sacred, remain
unconquered
within.

Let these letters in their strange assortment rise,
free from stoplights and schedules,
news casts and neighborhoods,
and become the great-winged thing
that thrusts us forward and upward,
to a future we call blessed, to that
inconceivable place where we are reborn.

Ysabel de la Rosa
Wichita Falls, Texas

Moment of Inertia

Left, then right; left, then right;
the groundskeeper sweeps
the nozzle of the blower
from side to side,
painting the green pavement gray.
The baby's swing softly
ticks back and forth
and the pendulum
of the mantel clock
counts down the days.
So different from the blade
of grass quivering in the wind.
But a world apart from
the homeless woman standing
on the verge of the busy street,
frozen in place on a sizzling August day.
She dreamily hums a favorite song
to the beat of her heart and
the pulses of the passing cars.

Stephen Sanders
Denton, Texas

Kaleidoscope

Forests and rivers, glaciers and oceans
Particles and neurons, human emotion
Swirls a kaleidoscope of beauty so wide
Sometimes I pause and tremble inside
May I understand what I clasp in my hand
A planet in need with people who bleed
Flowers today could wither away
Now I am living, so I will pray

All of my senses, all my emotion
May they bring me closer, put me in motion
To a kaleidoscope of beauty so wide
Sometimes I pause and tremble inside
May I feel the joy, may I hope may I grieve
Give me compassion, let me believe
Even my sadness, anger, and fear
Drawing me closer, drawing me near

Sometimes a fire, sometimes a light
Sometimes living water, like stars in the night
Swirls a kaleidoscope of all that's inside me
Feelings that swell like waves of the sea
May my arms embrace, may I feel in my face
Laughter and tears and a love that is near
Beauty so vast and beauty so wide
Sometimes I pause and tremble inside

Keith Sanford
Woodway, Texas

New Dawn

On the shore of Lake Limestone,
the early morning sun
catches a glint off the wings
of a slowly cruising bird.
The calm gray water
reflects a slight orange hue.
I'm still in shadows
where scattered trees
ease into the day.
Two days past full,
high above the opposite shore,
the moon is a bright white
with the standard gray patches
reflecting its peaks and valleys.
The moon passed over us all night,
the course it has taken for ages,
a welcome sight in the clear sky.
It seems on a journey
while we bask in the serenity
of a new dawn.

Stephen Schwei
Houston, Texas

Whenever It Smells Like Rain

Fresh stature is the grass after it,
knowing the downpour reaches the dirt
facing burial, then resurrection
as eager dew hangs along for the ride.

It slows down the city it feels like,
The coffeeshops are at a steady hum
Keeping the windows clear is a hard one
For they fog whenever the steamer is on.

Hunter boots and North Faces
Arise from the closet of moths nearly instantly,
As the clouds shun
the sun, yet still somewhere.

Laptops close on the subway,
As books resurge from old backpacks and purses
there's no wi-fi in here anyway.
They turn the old pages of pressed paper
Whenever it smells like rain.

Fiera M. Smith
Dallas, Texas

My Father's Woodpile

My father cuts his firewood, his chain saw smokes and
spits
Though he's four years past fourscore, a lot of wood is
split
Beneath the searing midday sun his energy is waning
Still he stalks the timber, intent and uncomplaining

Sweat pours off in rivulets, wood chips pierce his skin
Though covered in shavings, he stacks it to his chin
I wonder why his woodpile never seems diminished
Every time I visit his work is never finished

Then in an epiphany, it's all precise and clear
Why, when the day is oven-hot, he'll gamely persevere
Whoever hears my father's prayers would never take a
man
With an abundant woodpile stacked by his own hand

He fights to free his jammed-up saw; soon it's extricated
Once more he attacks the log, his purpose unabated
I view this self-reliant man who never seems defeated
And wonder: Can I face the day his woodpile is
depleted?

Nick Sweet
Shepherd, Texas

Submission

I never knew a river could be lassoed like a
wild horse, but he mighty Columbia River
twists and turns until it spills into the Pacific,
is dammed and cabled like a raging stallion
choked into submission by the end of a rope.
Chinook Indians once caught wild salmon
in their seines as the tenacious fish fought their
way upstream through the rushing water.

Today, sail surfers flower the Columbia like
butterflies, a sight to embellish as the river
roars and dances almost like it did when Lewis
and Clark first laid eyes upon it.

The Columbia retains its beauty,
like the caged zoo animal still exhibits his splendor,
but there is something sad about altering nature.

Sharon Taylor
Longview, Texas

While Folding Laundry at the Beach

Home misses me.
She stays behind,
content to tend the hydrangea-banked north side,
curate the collage of hallway portraits,
monitor the settling night noises.

The back bedroom phone rings now and again
with its mechanical message reply,
the long stretches of silence
chipped by occasional chatter from the grey cockatiel.

Home perks up midafternoon
at the postman's front porch clank,
and notes the piles of mail scattered across the dinner
table.
Home sees the cat meow through the dark kitchen,
nibbling the tuna treats the sitter leaves in her bowl.

Home watches,
faithfully
until the evening a suitcase
packed with a souvenir watercolor
returns, scraping
across the wooden bedroom floor
flooding the house with light.

Carol Thompson
Tyler, Texas

Sleeping In
(A Visit to the Grandparents)

The sheets smelled full of sunshine,
Where the wind had blown them through.
The soft quilt, made of old cloth,
Was completed and called new.
The temperature, just perfect,
Left each muscle deep in rest.
The thought of no alarm clock
Was the part that seemed the best.

Farm news on the radio
Gently overran the room,
And percolated coffee,
Became morning's new perfume.
Whispers of conversation,
And a light on down the hall,
Someone might be sleeping in,
But certainly not all.

Marlene Tucker
Axtell, Texas

Rekindle

Watch the ember kindle
Watch your dreams fade away
Follow the signs
To get through your day
Before you fall asleep
You see a bright flash
The ember sparks
A sacred ash
Watch your dreams return
Like a rekindling flame
Ease your mind
As the fire engraves a name
Forever burned deep in your mind
The name of a person
It will forever rewind
Each time you fall to slumber
The fire burns longer and longer
Until one night
Your dreams come true
When you realize that person
Lays beside you

Spencer Vansyckle
Waco, Texas

Japanese Print: Owl on Magnolia Branch
Circa 1870 – 1920

The lettering trails off into loops, squiggles —
the raptor, drifting in and out of a dream,
has trouble completing the poem.
A plump hare romps through his hopes.
He suppresses a memory of first flight.
How many nestlings vied for food?
In his prime, how sharp his senses,
how quickly, quietly he descended upon prey.
He owned the night.
It's as if the blooms have swallowed
his pink springtime.

Sylvia Riojas Vaughn
Plano, Texas

The First Juneteenth

... former slaves tossing their ragged garments into the creeks and rivers to adorn clothing taken from the plantations belonging to their former 'masters'.—Juneteenth.Com

After freedom rose from the fire,
after the news rolled onto Galveston beach,
after the winding plantation exodus,
some freed slaves sloughed their tattered clothes
from their bodies like dead skin.

Tossing those rags into the Gulf of Mexico,
they paced the banks, witnessed their past
sink into the swamp of the unknown.
Did anyone salvage a cuff, a pocket, a yoke?
Even the unsolved cradles a period
somewhere in its mystery.
Oh, to eavesdrop on gossiping gar
overshadowed by cotton.

***

Maybe this is freedom—
to shoulder the pain of others,
gather remnants, together.
Maybe freedom is a river
each of us can step into daily,
rid ourselves of what no longer fits.
Maybe water is to sacrifice what silence is
to dignity—
so the vulnerable walk without shame.

Loretta Diane Walker
Odessa, Texas

Till Death Do Us Part, or Not

When Black Widow
marries Bluebeard,
stalemate ensues.
Annihilation is now each lover's bleak intent.

Strikes, and parries,
counter every first;
stealth is on alert.
Every tender hook bleeds more lies than truth.

Within their ragged domicile
serrated pleasantries
cling to peppered walls
and silvered chards adorn each porcelain plate.

Secure in their combative
skills, each discounts
that over time
endless bouts without relief obscures the obvious.

They have grown old! Rusty
armor fans fatigue. Nasty
jabs have no heft, and to
their mutual horror, a single grave awaits the pair.

Germaine Welch
Houston, Texas

Bummer Fashionista

I fell apart inside a suit and tie
little at a time sprinkled in
pocket square sized bits
all over Dallas
It felt like adventure
packing to leave
like hopping train cars or
being poor in New York City
but those are just
the screens and songs
and you already know
being poor hurts anywhere
so surrender to your city
you'll never make it anywhere else
not with your defective mind
and don't look surprised
when you wake up
alone in years still here
and when you finally get fired
don't make them lie when you ask
how it is they saw through your masks
you never did wear disorder well
but damned if it doesn't go with everything.

David G. Williams III
Dallas, Texas

Take Time to Smell the Roses!

WE MEET IN THE H E B
as we have met @demonstrations and @musical events
over years and trends and storms
She is sniffing @the flowers.
"The white ones smell best!" (she shares)
So I stop sampling strawberries, and turn my attention
to the white daisies (refreshing!)
stargazer lilies (solemn!)
and all the various aromas emanating from these
bustling shelves of flowers
She warns me against the dyed flowers. I concur.
She is biased towards Texan flowers
so I follow her in taste sniffing every indigenous flower
bursting in light rain Austin happiness.
Then, like a miracle, she is gone, leaving me alone
among the strawberries
So (of course) I open their lid, take a deep sniff
and smile strawberry smiles all around the H E B...

Thom Woodruff
Austin, Texas

Fruit of the Vine...

Her painted gourds hung from sinewy vines
bent into shape by weight and hard years
and the whims of the artist's brush, the length
and weight of the twine that held them
seedless now and polished by the wind.

They made music, held a song that only
the wind pulled from them in its restless
journey at the edge of the river bank
where now and then one gourd would hit
another, and unlikely applause occurred.

They were ancient gourds, from a vine
no longer remembered, planted by a hand
attached to no name, and when asked, we
would just say "no one remembers, no one
cared until someone painted the first one."

June Zaner
Houston, Texas

Birds

Some birds just look like that:
    Gulls perhaps, or gangly white ibis
With thin penciled wings, light
    Tendrils waving gracefully behind
Curved beaks, soft heads cocked for flight
    Feathers tight, wings spread as if
There were no need of wind or even
    Air to billow hollow bones.

Aloft! These lithe birds fly! leaving
    Their peculiar stains, their marks
Below, easy droppings flung from any
    Seven-storied perch, where they alight
First one then others flinting down
To any branch, wire or ledge up high enough
    To contemplate the scene below:

Strange creatures, they carouse
    The skies, eyes alert and lean:
Centurions of debris and other scattered things.

Richard Zaner
Houston, Texas

WordFest 2017 Feature Poet

Karla K. Morton (Fort Worth, Texas)
The 2010 Texas Poet Laureate and a member and
Councilor of the Texas Institute of Letters is a celebrated
poet, author, speaker and photographer. A Betsy Colquitt
Award winner, a two-time Indie Book Award Winner, a
North Texas Book Festival Award winner and a nominee
for the National Cowgirl Hall of Fame, she has been
widely published in literary journals and is the author of
eleven books of poetry: *Wee Cowrin' Timorous Beastie*
(a 17th Century Scottish epic book/CD created in
collaboration with award-winning composer Howard
Baer); *Becoming Superman* (Rogers Publishing/Wheeler
Press); *Redefining Beauty*, a journey through cancer
diagnosis, chemo, radiation and recovery (Dos Gatos
Press, 3rd printing); *Stirring Goldfish*, a Sufi poetry book
(Finishing Line Press); *Names We've Never Known*
(Texas Review Press); *Karla K. Morton: New and
Selected Poems* (TCU Press); *Passion, Art, Community:
Denton, Texas in Word and Image* (the City of Denton,
Texas); *8 Voices: Contemporary Poetry from the
American Southwest*, a collaborate work written by
Morton and seven other prominent contemporary poets
in the American southwest (Baskerville Publishing);
*Hometown, Texas: Young Poets and Artists Celebrate
Their Roots* (TCU Press); *Constant State of Leaping*
(Texas Review Press); and *Accidental Origami* (Texas
Review Press). Another book, *No End of Vision: Texas
as Seen by Two Laureates*, features Ms. Morton's black
and white photography combined with poetry written by
2005 Texas Poet Laureate Alan Birkelbach. A traveling
photography and poetry exhibit by the same name is also
being shown in museums and galleries throughout Texas
(and beyond). Described as "one of the more
adventurous voices in American poetry," Ms. Morton

has been featured on Good Morning Texas, NPR, ABC News, CBS News and in countless newspapers, blogs and magazines. She is frequently invited to present as a keynote speaker at conventions, conferences, bookstores, universities, festivals, and schools. An avid photographer, Morton has also had many showings of her black and white artwork, has been nominated for the honor of the Texas 2D Artist and loves to mix poetry with other art forms. Morton was born in Fort Worth, holds a Journalism degree from Texas A&M University and currently resides in Fort Worth, Texas.

Karla K. Morton

Ann Howells

WordFest Workshop Presenter

Ann Howells has edited *Illya's Honey* for eighteen years, recently taking it digital: www.IllyasHoney.com. Her publications are: *Black Crow in Flight* (Main Street Rag), *Under a Lone Star* (Village Books), *Letters for My Daughter* (Flutter), and *Cattlemen & Cadillacs* (Dallas Poets Communities), an anthology of D/FW poets she edited. Her chapbook manuscript, *Softly Beating Wings*, won the William D. Barney Memorial Chapbook Contest 2017. When not involved in poetry, she likes to photograph Texas courthouses and spoil her dogs.

Ann's poetry appears widely in small press and university publications (over 300) here and abroad including *Spillway, THEMA, San Pedro River Review, Concho River Review, Little Patuxent Review, Crannog* (Ireland), *and Magma* (England). She has work in the anthologies: *Goodbye, Mexico* and *The Southern Poetry Anthology, Volume VIII: Texas* (Texas Review Press), *Pushing the Envelope,* and *Texas Weather Anthology* (Lamar University Press). Ann served as President of Dallas Poets Community for four years and as Treasurer for many more. In 2001, she was named a "Distinguished Poet of Dallas" by the city. She serves on advisory boards and panels for various literary organizations, serves as a judge for poetry competitions, and is a member of the team that takes poetry into the schools, elementary through college. She has received four Pushcart nominations.

WordFest Workshop Presenters

Joyce Gullickson lives in Sun City, Texas with her husband, Mike. She works as a Registered Nurse while following the true desire of her heart to write poetry. She believes poetry has the ability to uplift and unite us, promoting change. Joyce has been published in Sunscripts, AIPF's di-vêrsé-city, the Texas Poetry Calendar and When Time and Space Conspire. She co-edits the Enigmatist, with her husband Mike; and Blue Hole, a poetry chapbook of the Georgetown Poetry Festival. Joyce and Mike host 'Poetry Aloud' an open mic at the Georgetown Public Library every second and fourth Saturday.

Michael Gullickson has published poems in the San Antonio Express, The Via Bus System, Barnwood Press, Affirming Flame, and The Texas Poetry Calendar, among others. His poem 'A Promise of Music' won First Place and the right to call himself Senior Poet Laureate in 2009. With his wife they publish The Enigmatist as well as Blue Hole magazine. For submission guidelines contact poetkind@yahoo.com. They also host the Georgetown Poetry Festival in October. His book, *A Promise of Music*, is now available on Amazon.

WordFest Anthology Editor

Sandi Horton (Woodway, Texas) is passionate about writing and performing poetry and music. She served for many years on the board of directors for the Cultural Arts of Waco, parent organization to the Waco Cultural Arts Fest, and is a four-time chairperson for WordFest. Her work has appeared in Langdon Review of the Arts in Texas, di-vêrsé-city, Blue Hole, Art of Peace, Animal Tales, American Recorder Journal, and many other publications. Her three books are *My House of Poetry*, *Cooking Without Recipes*, and *Where is Yonder?* Sandi has been selected to be the '2018 Writer in Residence' for the Langdon Review of the Arts in Texas. She studied at the C.G. Jung Institute of Psychology in Zurich, Switzerland for the 2017 Winter Intensive. She enjoys performing jazz, world music, and Native American music. She and her husband Jeff have recorded four albums as the HORTON DUO and have over 420 archived concerts. Sandi holds a B.M.E. (music) from Texas Tech and M.S. (Ed Psych) from Baylor. She was a counselor for 15 years, and served four years as a band/orchestra director in public schools. In September 2016, Sandi Horton co-founded the HOT (Heart of Texas) Poets Society, a member chapter of the Poetry Society of Texas (PST). She is the chairperson for the 2018 PST State Conference to be held in Waco.

WordFest Committee 2017

Sandi Horton, chairperson
Doreen Ravenscroft, festival director
Chris Boldt
Jeff Horton

Details about **WordFest** can be found on our Facebook page at www.facebook.com/wacoartsfest.org

Information about the **Waco Cultural Arts Fest** can be found at www.wacoartsfest.org, or on Facebook at www.facebook.com/WacoCulturalArtsFestival.

Thank you to our WordFest sponsors!

REDFIN

Texas
Commission
on the Arts

ART WORKS.

National Endowment for the Arts
arts.gov

76763328R10052